U0754728

2024 年长白山入选世界地质公园

大美长白山

Great Beauty of Mt. Changbaishan

卓永生　孙　志 / 主编

吉林科学技术出版社

为守护美丽地球
贡献长白山力量

Embracing the Might of Mt. Changbaishan
Safeguarding the Splendor of Earth

作为中国火山之王，长白山独特的火山地质地貌具有重要的科研价值，是研究地球演化历史、揭示地球生物形成演变的重要材料和论据，对研究我国东部新生代火山形成的动力机制、火山灾害监测与预防都具有重要的现实意义。保障和改善长白山区域内的生态环境，提高生态质量、建设生态文明，对于整个东北地区的生态平衡和经济社会发展都将起到无可替代的重要作用。

长白山的保护和发展经历了相当长的历史阶段，从1960年成立长白山自然保护区，到1979年被联合国教科文组织批准列为"人与生物圈计划"世界生物圈保护区，再到2009年建立国家地质公园，几代长白山人经过不懈努力和积极探索，走出了一条适合本区域资源保护与经济发展协同的健康发展之路。2005年6月，长白山保护开发区管理委员会成立后，始终坚持以国际化的生态文明视野谋划战略布局，全力守护系统完整的自然生态，精心打造人与自然和谐相处的度假胜地和"生态天堂"。

As the "King of volcanoes" in China, Mt. Changbaishan unique volcanic geological landform possesses significant scientific research value, serving as an indispensable material and evidence for studying the history of earth evolution and unraveling the formation and evolution of earth organisms. It has important practical significance for exploring the dynamic mechanism of the formation of Cenozoic volcanoes in the eastern China, as well as for volcanic disaster monitoring and prevention. Therefore, the ongoing commitment to safeguarding and enhancing the ecological environment of the Mt. Changbaishan region, along with the unwavering focus on elevating ecological quality and fostering ecological civilization, holds a pivotal and irreplaceable significance in preserving ecological balance and driving economic and social progress throughout Northeast China.

The protection and development of Mt. Changbaishan have undergone significant historical stages. Since its Nature Reserve was launched in 1960, Mt. Changbaishan was approved by UNESCO as a world biosphere reserve of the "Man and the Biosphere Program" in 1979, and successively a national geopark was established in 2009. After several generations' unremitting efforts and active exploration, a development path has been found for the coordinated and healthy development of resource protection and economic growth in this region. In June 2005, following the establishment of Mt. Changbaishan Protection and Development Zone Management Committee, efforts have consistently been made to orchestrate strategic layouts from an international ecological civilization vision, vigorously safeguarding the integrity of the natural ecosystem, and meticulously building a resort and

2020年，秉承联合国教科文组织世界地质公园"颂造化之神奇、谋区域之常兴"的理念，长白山保护开发区管理委员会启动世界地质公园创建工作。按照联合国教科文组织世界地质公园的标准和要求，着力构建科学合理的管理体系，不断优化完善和保护基础设施、科研监测设施及旅游服务设施，深入开展地质科研科普，积极推动社区参与和发展，地质公园建设工作取得显著成效。2020年10月，长白山保护开发区向联合国教科文组织提交了世界地质公园申请报告。2023年7月，联合国教科文组织世界地质公园秘书处派出考察评估组，到长白山开展实地考察评估。2024年3月，长白山被联合国教科文组织批准列为"世界地质公园"，

"ecological paradise" where man and nature live in harmony.

In 2020, adhering to the concept of UNESCO Global Geoparks—celebrating the wonders of nature and seeking the prosperity of the region, Mt. Changbaishan Protection and Development Zone Management Committee launched the development of the Global Geopark. In accordance with the standards and requirements of the UNESCO Global Geoparks, efforts have been focused on constructing a scientifically sound management system, continuously optimizing and improving infrastructure for protection, research monitoring and tourist services. Extensive geological research and public outreach have been conducted, together with actively community involvement and development being promoted. With concerted efforts, significant progress has been made in the construction of the Geopark. In October 2020, an application report for the Global Geopark was submitted to UNESCO. In July 2023, the Secretariat of UNESCO Global Geoparks sent an inspection and evaluation team to Mt. Changbaishan for on-site inspection and evaluation. In March 2024, Mt. Changbaishan Geopark was approved by UNESCO

这是长白山保护开发区发展史上具有里程碑意义的一件大事，也是继获得联合国教科文组织世界生物圈保护区、世界自然保护联盟绿色名录"最佳自然保护区"后，长白山走向世界的又一张国际名片。在世界地质公园品牌影响下，长白山在珍贵地质遗迹保护、促进科学普及和区域可持续性发展等方面翻开崭新一页。

长白山作为东北地区最高水塔，长白山水源滋养了广袤的东北大地。跻身世界地质公园，长白山进一步融入世界自然和文化保护大家庭，成为承担与全球共同呵护自然、传承文明的一员，这必将为共筑美丽中国梦，弘扬地质公园文化魅力，守护地球美丽家园绿水青山贡献长白山力量。

as a "Global Geopark". This milestone event in the development history of the Mt. Changbaishan Protection and Development Zone signifies another international recognition following its designation as a UNESCO Global Biosphere Reserve and a Best Nature Reserve on the Green List of the World Conservation Union. Under the influence of the brand of the Global Geopark, Mt. Changbaishan has ushered in a new chapter in the protection of precious geological relics, promoting scientific popularization and regional sustainable development.

As the tallest water tower in Northeast China, Mt. Changbaishan nourishes the vast land. By joining the ranks of UNESCO Global Geoparks, Mt. Changbaishan further integrates into the global family of natural and cultural protection, and has become a member committed to protecting nature and inheriting civilization together with the world. All these efforts will certainly contribute to making the Beautiful Chinese Dream a reality, promoting the cultural charm of geoparks, and safeguarding the green mountains and clear water of our beloved planet.

目 录 | CONTENTS

巨型复式火山锥
Huge Composite Volcanic Cone

长白山火山是目前世界上保存最完整的晚新生代（约1,120,000年前—1,000年前）多成因复合巨型火山锥之一，火山先后经历了以溢流喷发造盾为主、火山喷发造锥次之、最后强烈爆发的多期火山活动，最后一次大规模的喷发为1,000年前的普林尼式大爆发。火山锥体平面上呈椭圆形，长约27千米，宽约14千米，由白云峰、天文峰等16座山峰和刃形山脊环抱而构成完好巨大的火山口，最高海拔2,749.2米。

长白山世界地质公园的地质遗迹类型主要包括以巨型复式火山锥、火山口群为代表的火山地貌，以千年火山大喷发及其形成的碎屑流层、空落浮岩层为代表的火山喷发碎屑堆积——火山碎屑峡谷景观，以及以天池为代表的水体景观。

The volcano of Mt. Changbaishan is one of the best well-preserved late Cenozoic (about 1,120,000 to 1,000 years ago) huge multi-genetic and composite volcanic cone in the world. Having successively undergone the initiative shield-building through effusive eruption, followed by cones after volcanic eruptions, the volcano eventually entered the last explosive eruption stage. In other words, there are multiple periods of volcanic activities, and the latest large-scale eruption was the Plinian eruption 1,000 years ago. The volcanic cone's surface is elliptically shaped, stretching about 27 kilometers in length and 14 kilometers in width. The huge complete crater, with a maximum altitude of 2,749.2 meters, is surrounded by 16 peaks (such as Peak Baiyun and Astronomy Peak) and blade-shaped ridges.

The main geoheritage types in Mt. Changbaishan UNESCO Global Geopark primarily include volcanic landforms dominated by the huge composite volcanic cone and crater clusters, pyroclastic accumulations represented by millennia-old volcanic eruptions and their resulting debris flow and airfall pumice layers, pyroclastic gorge landscapes, as well as waterscape symbolized by Lake Tianchi (literally meaning "summit crater lake").

长白山天池

Lake Tianchi of Mt. Changbaishan

长白山火山破火山口蓄水成湖，名为天池。天池水面海拔高度2,194米，是中国海拔最高和面积最大的火山口湖，水域面积近9.4平方千米，水域边界周长13.33千米，湖水最深373.2米，蓄水量达19.88×10^{8}立方米，水面和环形峰脊的最大高差达500余米。火山口最终形成于千年前的大爆发，湖水主要由地下水补给。

The volcanic crater of Mt. Changbaishan collects water to form a lake, known as Lake Tianchi. With a water altitude of 2,194 meters, LakeTianchi is the highest and largest crater lake in China, covering an area of nearly 9.4 square kilometers and a shoreline perimeter of 13.33 kilometers. The maximum depth of the lake is 373.2 meters, with a water volume of approximately 19.88×10^{8} cubic meters. The maximum height gap between the water surface and the annular peak ridge is over 500 meters. The volcanic crater was ultimately formed after a massive eruption thousands years ago, with the lake primarily replenished by underground water.

斗转星移——池南景区天池星空

The shifting of the stars and the rotation of the Dipper - the starry sky of Lake Tianchi in Chinan area

天池日出
Sunrise of Lake Tianchi

观日峰：天池内侧的断崖与倒石堆
Sun Observing Peak: the cliffs and talus piles on the inner side of Lake Tianchi

天文峰：火山碎屑岩与火山灰
Astronomy Peak: volcanic clasolite and volcanic ash

卧虎峰与青石峰：风化水蚀塑造千姿百态
Crouching Tiger Peak and Bluestone Peak: various shapes sculpted by weathering and water erosion

天池北麓：凝灰岩与火山碎屑岩
Northern foot of Lake Tianchi: tuff and volcanic clasolite

Mt. Changbaishan

春日长白山
Mt. Changbaishan in spring

佛光
Buddhist light

日落铁壁峰：从主峰向山下望去，茫茫林海生机勃勃，覆盖在熔岩台地之上

Sunset Iron Wall Peak: when looking down from the main peak, one is greeted by a sprawling and
vibrant forest, blanketing the lava plateau below

乘槎河口两侧的滑坡体

Landslides at both sides of Chengcha River estuary

天池主峰周边风化形成的阶坎和鳞片

Terraces and scales formed by weathering around the main peak of Lake Tianchi

芝盘峰：风化地貌，巨型黑曜石
Zhipan Peak: weathered landforms and giant obsidian

长白山北坡：发育壮观的柱状节理

North slope of Mt. Changbaishan: spectacular columnar fractures

长白山北坡：发育壮观的柱状节理
North slope of Mt.Changbaishan: spectacular columnar fractures

天文峰：天池内侧的断崖与倒石堆

Astronomy Peak: the cliffs and talus piles on the inner side of Lake Tianchi

芝盘峰：天池内侧冰缘地貌

Zhipan Peak: periglacial landforms on the inner side of Lake Tianchi

古冰川冰缘地貌

Periglacial Landform of Ancient Glaciers

长白山火山锥体由于气候高寒，融冻和雪蚀作用明显，处于现代冰缘环境，形成了许多不同类型的冰缘地貌形态。虽然分布并不广泛，但在气候地貌研究上具有重要意义。其中主要有倒石堆、石海、石流坡、雪蚀洼地、雪蚀岩龛、草皮坡坎、石川、石多边形、石带和热融洼地等。

Due to the frigid climate characterized by frost-thaw and snow erosion, the volcanic cones of Mt. Changbaishan have given rise to a diverse array of periglacial landforms in a modern periglacial environment. Although not widely distributed, these landforms hold significant importance in climatic geomorphology research. The prominent examples of these landforms include talus piles, ground moraine, rock slope, snow-eroded depressions, snow-eroded niches, turf-covered slopes, glacial till, stone polygons, stone bands, and thermokarst depressions.

倾斜熔岩高原
Oblique Lava Plateau

　　倾斜熔岩高原为熔岩台地与巨型火山锥的过渡地貌类型，环带形分布于火山锥体周围，平均宽度20千米，海拔1,100～1,700米，坡度3°～5°，发育有高密度的河流，是东北地区"三江"（松花江、图们江和鸭绿江）的源头区。熔岩高原主要由玄武岩组成，其上发育寄生小火山锥体和未被熔岩淹没的侵蚀残丘，与下面的熔岩台地接触处坡度有明显变化。

　　The oblique lava plateau represents a transitional landform between the alpine lava plateau and huge volcanic cones. Spanning an average width of 20 kilometers, with an altitude ranging from 1,100 meters to 1,700 meters, and a slope of 3° to 5°, the oblique lava plateau encircles the volcanic cones in a ring-like fashion. Characterized by a dense network of rivers, this region serves as the source area of the "Three Rivers" (Songhua River, Tumen River and Yalu River) in Northeast China. The oblique lava plateau is mainly composed of basalt, on which small volcanic cones and erosion remnants not submerged by lava are developed. There is a noticeable change in slope at the contact point between the lava plateau and the underlying terrain.

长白山U型谷：长白山经历了多次冰川刻蚀，是中国东部晚更新世以来存在冰川作用的典型山地之一

U-shaped valley of Mt. Changbaishan: Mt. Changbaishan has undergone multiple episodes of glacial erosion, making it one of the typical mountainous areas in eastern China where glacial action has been present since the late Pleistocene

U型谷：流纹质碱性粗面岩
U-shaped valley: rhyolite and alkali trachyte

西麓U型槽谷与流水侵蚀的切沟

U-shaped valley and gully subjected to water erosion on the western foot

高山苔原：流水侵蚀与浮石岩
Alpine tundra: water erosion and pumice rock

老虎背下缘：受流水侵蚀的火山灰
Lower edge of the tiger's back: volcanic ash subjected to water erosion

高山苔原带
Alpine tundra zone

南麓：海拔2,200米以上的高山苔原，远处为浮石岩
Southern foot: alpine tundra above 2,200 meters, with pumice rocks in the distance

聚龙温泉群
Julong Hot Spring Cluster

聚龙温泉
Julong Hot Spring

温泉群
Hot Spring Cluster

地质公园内有数十个地下热水溢出点构成的温泉群，其中以聚龙温泉最具代表性。聚龙温泉属于高热火山自溢温泉，在1,000多平方米范围内有47个泉眼，水温平均70℃，最高可达82℃，日涌热水总量6,500吨，pH值为7.5～7.7。泉水含有硫化物、偏硅酸等多种物质，具有较高的医疗价值。另外，比较著名的温泉有锦江温泉、湖滨温泉以及芦泉、仙人桥温泉群、十八道沟温泉、玉浆泉和药水泉等。温泉指数是监测长白山火山活动的重要依据，具有重大的科学研究、科学普及和实际应用价值。

There are dozens of underground hot water vents within the geopark, which form a hot spring cluster, with Julong Hot Spring being the most representative. Julong Hot Spring belongs to high-temperature volcanic-derived spring, with 47 spring vents within an area of over 1,000 square meters. The average water temperature is 70℃, reaching up to 82℃ at its highest, with a daily flow of 6,500 tons of hot water and a pH value around 7.5 to 7.7. The spring water contains various trace elements with significant medical value, such as hydrogen sulfide and silicic acid. Other well-known hot springs include Jinjiang Hot Spring, Hubin Hot Spring, as well as Luquan, Xianrenqiao Hot Spring Cluster, Shibadaogou Hot Spring, Yujiang Spring, and Yaoshui Spring. The hot spring index serves as an important basis for monitoring volcanic activity in Mt. Changbaishan, providing substantial value for scientific research, education, and practical applications.

天池湖滨温泉

Hot spring of Tianchi lakeside

锦江温泉
Jinjiang Hot Spring

小天池

Little Lake Tianchi

　　由于长白山火山为多口喷发火山，因而形成了大小不一、形状各异、深浅有别的多个火山口湖。

　　小天池周长260米，面积约5,380平方米，水深10余米，只有进水口没有出水口，所以池水终年不枯，令人称奇，这与地下水补给有关。水面略呈圆环状，故又称"银环湖"。

Mt. Changbaishan volcano, characterized by multi-vent eruptions, has given rise to several crater lakes of varying sizes, shapes, and depths.

Little Lake Tianchi boasts a perimeter of 260 meters, an area of approximately 5,380 square meters, and a depth of over 10 meters. Despite having only an inlet without any outlet, the lake maintains its water levels year-round, a remarkable phenomenon attributed to underground water replenishment. Its slightly ring-shaped water surface has earned it the moniker "Silver Ring Lake."

小天池
Little Lake Tianchi

小天池
Little Lake Tianchi

圆池
Lake Yuanchi

王　池

Lake Wangchi

　　王池属于较典型的低平火山口湖，湖近于圆形，直径约140米，有明显的火山口缘。口缘高出地面4米，环绕王池一周，口缘内坡度50°左右，水深未知。环湖四周植被繁茂，风景宜人。

　　Lake Wangchi (literally meaning king's pool) is a typical low-lying volcanic crater lake. The lake is nearly circular in shape with a diameter of about 140 meters, and has a distinct volcanic crater rim. The rim, encircling the lake, is 4 meters higher than the ground. The inner slope of the rim is about 50°, and the depth of the water is unknown. Dense vegetation, which is nestled within a sprawling garden of thousands of acres, surrounds the lake and creates a picturesque landscape.

流水地貌

Fluvial Landform

　　以长白山中心火山锥和望天鹅盾形火山锥为原点，分别形成两个大型放射状水系。水系流入熔岩台地后，逐渐汇合，形成稀疏的树枝状水系。本区的地貌侵蚀发育还处于幼年阶段，水系还未充分发育，河网密度较小，地面比较完整，谷间地宽广平坦，保存着大片原始熔岩地貌。河流以侵蚀、搬运作用为主，堆积作用甚弱。有许多幢谷子、隘谷，主要见于槽子河、梯子河、锦江、松江河、二道白河、三道白河等河流的上游。

　　Centered on the volcanic cone of Mt. Changbaishan and the shield-shaped volcanic cone of Wangtian'e, two large radial water systems have been developed respectively. After the water systems enter the lava plateaus, they gradually converge and develop into a sparse dendritic system. The geomorphic erosion in this area is still in its infancy, with the river systems not fully developed and a relatively low river network density. The ground surface is relatively intact, with wide and flat valleys preserving a large area of original lava landforms. The rivers are mainly dominated by erosion and transportation, with deposition being significantly limited. There are many narrow valleys and gorges, mainly found in the upstream of rivers such as Caozi River, Tizi River, Jinjiang, Songjiang River, Erdaobaihe, and Sandaobaihe.

冬日瀑布：雪量大和雪期长是造成雪蚀的动力来源
Winter waterfall: heavy snowfall and long snow duration provide the driving force for snow erosion

瀑布两侧形成的坡积裙
Skirt-like slope deposit formed on both sides of the waterfall

长白瀑布

Changbai Waterfall

在1,250米长的乘槎河（松花江的源头）上游，源自天池的流水从断崖处跌落，飞流直下，形成了落差大、流速急的长白瀑布。瀑布落差68米，溅起数米高的飞浪，似烟如雾，景观怡人。长白瀑布的形成与地质构造关系密切，当乘槎河流水到达被横向延伸的地质断裂截断形成的断崖时，水流就沿着断裂面从高处向低处跌落，从而形成了令人叹为观止的长白瀑布。

Upstream along the Chengcha River, the source of the Songhua River, lies the magnificent Changbai Waterfall, also known as the perpetual Changbai Waterfall. Cascading down from the cliff's edge for a distance of 1,250 meters, the waterfall boasts an impressive drop of 68 meters. As the waterfall rushes downward with great speed, it generates towering waves and mist, creating a delightful spectacle. This picturesque waterfall is formed when the Chengcha River encounters a laterally extending fault, resulting in the formation of a cliff. Here, the water flows along the fault plane from a higher elevation to a lower one, shaping the breathtaking Changbai Waterfall.

绿渊潭

Green Abyss Pool

大戏台河：阶梯状跌水
Daxitai River: step-like waterfall

二道白河：山涧瀑布流水

Erdaobaihe: cascade and stream in the ravine

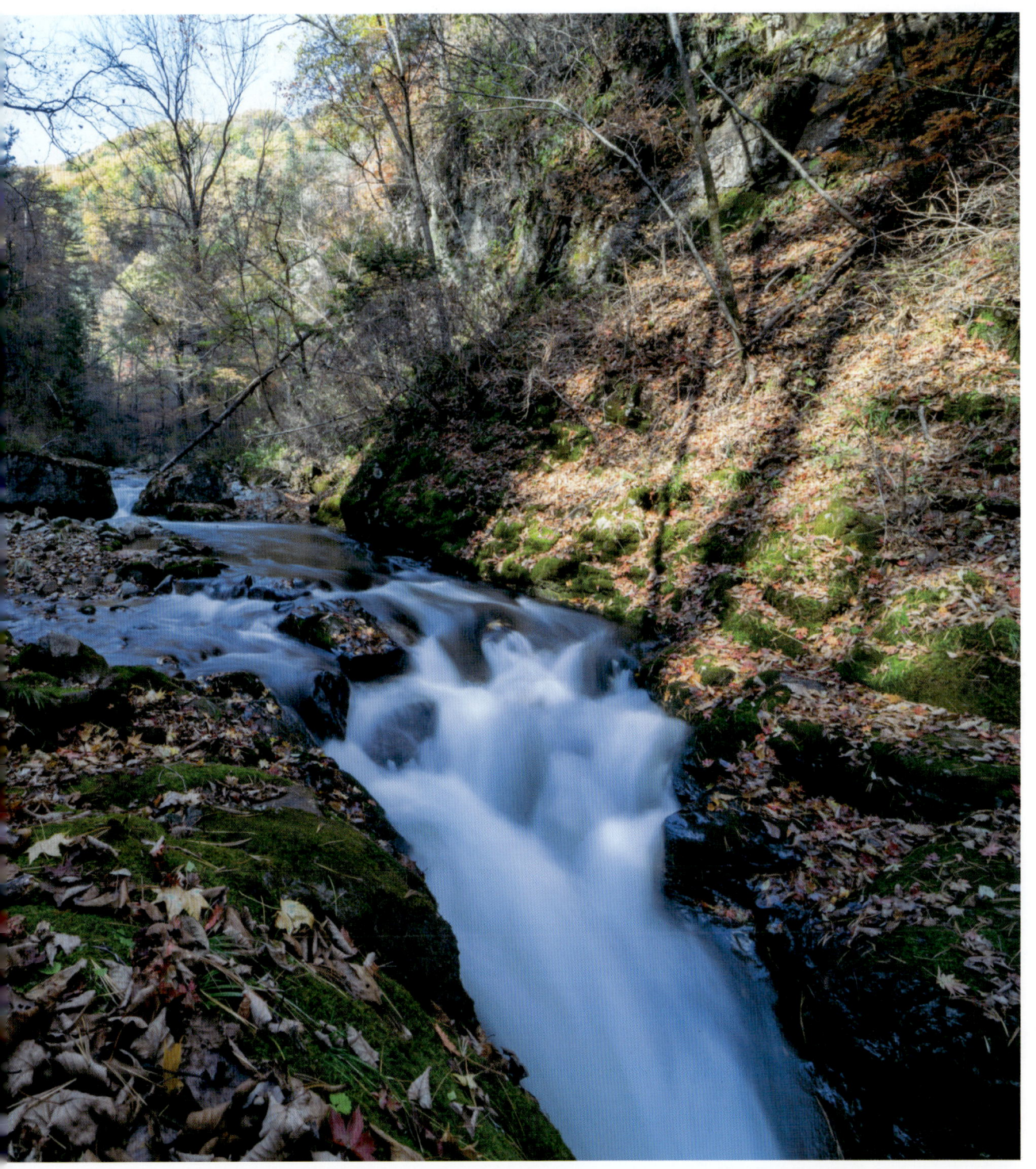

北麓秋溪：流水侵蚀的切沟
Autumn stream on the northern foot: gullies subjected to water erosion

森林流水地貌
Fluvial landform in forest

流水地貌
Fluvial landform

森林流水地貌
Fluvial landform in forest

药水江门坎：森林流水切割地貌

Yaoshuijiang Menkan: landform eroded by forest stream

北麓秋溪：森林中的水体景观
Autumn stream on the northern foot: waterscape in the forest

熔岩塌陷（谷底森林）

Lava Depression (Forest at Valley Bottom)

　　谷底森林是由于熔岩台地上熔岩塌陷，形成了三壁陡峭直立、深度达百米的塌陷洼地，塌陷三壁皆为巨厚层状玄武岩，形成的洼地宽约300米，长度延伸约3,000米。熔岩台地上的流水（松花江）沿熔岩缝隙下切数十米。塌陷洼地中植被覆盖，树林参天，称为"地下森林"。

　　The forest at the vally bottom is formed due to the collapse of lava on the lava plateau, creating steep and vertical collapsed depressions with depth of up to 100 meters. The walls of three sides are all composed of huge-bedded basalt, forming a depression of approximately 300 meters in width and extending about 3,000 meters in length. The water (Songhua River) on the lava plateau cuts down several tens of meters along the lava fissures. The collapsed depressions are covered with vegetation and towering forests, known as the "underground forest".

熔岩台地

Lava Plateau

　　熔岩是地下岩浆喷发到地面上冷凝形成的岩石，岩浆的流动性可以使其分布在较广的范围，形成熔岩台地，它是火山岩地区独特的地貌景观。长白山熔岩台地分布于海拔高度600～1,100米，主要由军舰山玄武质熔岩组成，地势广阔平坦，植被发育完整，是阔叶林和红松的主要分布区域。

　　Lava is a kind of volcanic rock formed by the condensation of underground magma erupted onto the surface of the earth. The fluidity of magma allows it to distribute over a wide area and form lava plateaus, which are unique geomorphic landscapes in volcanic regions. The lava plateaus of Mt. Changbaishan are distributed at an altitude of 600 meters to 1,100 meters, mainly composed of Junjianshan basaltic lava. The plateaus are vast and flat with well-developed vegetation, representing the main distribution area for broad-leaved forests and Red pine forests.

日照金山

Mt. Changbaishan bathed in sunshine

远眺长白山：玄武岩造盾形成熔岩台地

Panoramic view of Mt. Changbaishan: lava plateau formed by basaltic shield volcanoes

长白山火山熔岩台地是长白山自然保护区的重要组成部分，是各种珍稀动植物的家园，
素有"天然博物馆""物种基因库"的美誉

The volcanic lava plateau of Mt. Changbaishan, an important part of the Mt. Changbaishan Nature Reserve,

is home to various rare flora and fauna, which is renowned as a natural museum and a gene bank for species

北麓冬日远眺长白山

Panoramic view of Mt. Changbaishan from the northern foot in winter

西麓冬日远眺长白山
Panoramic view of Mt. Changbaishan from the western foot in winter

垂直景观

Vertical Landscape

　　长白山的垂直景观，相对高度约2,000米。在海拔1,100米以下为针阔混交林带和阔叶林带。当海拔到达1,100米，随着海拔升高，降水量增加，气温降低，依次形成针叶林带、岳桦林带和高山苔原带，呈明显的带状分布。山麓至山顶，不同的自然景观随着山势起伏而呈现出有层次的变换。游客从山脚到山顶，如同从欧亚大陆的温带跋涉到极地地区，各类植被景观可一览无余。

The vertical landscape of Mt.Changbaishan features a relative elevation of approximately 2,000 meters. Below an altitude of 1,100 meters, there are mixed forests of Red pines and broad-leaved trees, as well as broadleaved forests. As the altitude rises above 1,100 meters, the precipitation increases and the temperature decreases, giving rise to coniferous forests, alpine Betula ermanii forests, and alpine tundra, which exhibit a distinct zonal distribution. The natural landscapes vary distinctly from the foothills to the summit, showcasing layered transformations that correspond to the undulating contours of the mountains. Over a journey of several tens of kilometers, it feels like traversing from the temperate zone to the polar region of Eurasia, with all major landscapes in full view.

高山苔原带

Alpine Tundra Zone

　　海拔2,100米以上为高山苔原带，以极地植物区系成分为主，如由毛毡杜鹃、牛皮杜鹃、高山笃斯越橘、松毛翠等组成的低矮的小灌木群落等。

Alpine tundra zone in Mt. Changbaishan is above an altitude of 2,100 meters, where botanical species are mainly polar flora, dwarf shrubs such as rhododendron confertissimum, rhododendron aureum, bog blueberry, phyllodoce caerulea and etc.

岳桦林带

Birch Forest Zone

海拔1,700~2,100米为岳桦林带，代表树种是岳桦和偃松，由它们构成独特的矮曲林。少量云杉、冷杉也生长在此带。

The alpine birch forest is located at an altitude of 1,700 meters to 2,100 meters. The representative tree species are Betula ermanii and Pinus pumila, forming a unique elfin forest with a small number of spruces and firs.

针叶林带

Coniferous Forest Zone

　　海拔1,100~1,700米为针叶林带，南鄂霍次克植物区系成分增多，主要森林植被为鱼鳞云杉、臭冷杉，混有少量红松及黄花落叶松。

　　Located at an altitude of 1,100 meters to 1,700 meters, coniferous forest zone is characterized by an increasing number of flora species of South Okhotsk. The main forest vegetation consists of mixed coniferous forest of Picea jezoensis, Siberian white fir, and a few Red pines and Larix olgensis.

针阔混交林带

Mixed Coniferous Broad-leaved Forest Zone

海拔500~1,100米为针阔混交林带，属于长白山植物区系成分，主要森林植被是以红松为主的针阔叶混交林。该带是长白山区面积最广、生物种类最丰富的地区。

Located at an altitude of 500 meters to 1,100 meters, the mixed coniferous and broad-leaved forest is featured with the mixed forest of Red pine and broadleaved tree, which belongs to the Mt. Changbaishan flora. The main forest vegetation is dominated by Red pines. This zone is the most extensive and biologically diverse area in Mt. Changbaishan.

阔叶林带
Broadleaf Forest Zone

  海拔500米以下为阔叶林带，森林植被主要有蒙古栎、山杨、白桦、色木槭、椴树、榆树等。

  The deciduous broad-leaved forest belt is located below an altitude of 500 meters. The main botanical species are Mongolian Oak, Populus tremuloides, Silver Birth, Acer mono, linden, elm, etc.

牛皮杜鹃

Rhododendron aureum

海拔700米的熔岩台地火山灰上生长的美人松
Changbai Scotch pine growing on the lava platform covered with volcanic ash at an altitude of 700 meters

十五道沟：玄武岩柱状节理
Shiwudao Gou: basalt columnar fractures

火山碎屑峡谷地貌

Pyroclastic Gorge Landforms

　　锦江峡谷、鸭绿江峡谷、浮石林峡谷是长白山世界地质公园独有的高原火山碎屑峡谷地貌，是火山碎屑流层经流水侵蚀、切割形成的峡谷地貌，保存了长白山千年大喷发过程中形成的各类堆积物，是对喷发过程的详细记录，对火山爆炸式喷发序列的建立具有重要意义。峡谷中形成的石林、石柱、象形石等奇特微地貌景观，丰富了火山成因峡谷地貌的类型，在中国乃至世界范围内都十分罕见。

The Jinjiang Gorge, Yalu River Gorge, and Fushilin Gorge are unique plateau pyroclas tic debris gorge landscapes found in the Mt. Changbaishan UNESCO Global Geopark. They are formed by the erosion and cutting of pyroclastic flow layers by flowing water, preserving various deposits formed during the millennium-long eruption process of Mt. Changbaishan. They provide a detailed record of the eruption process and are of significant importance in establishing sequences of volcanic explosive eruptions. The peculiar micro-landscapes such as stone forests, stone pillars, and pictographic stones formed in the gorge enrich the types of volcanic origin gorge landscapes, which are extremely rare in China and even worldwide.

锦江峡谷：残留的岩柱

Jinjiang Gorge: remnant rock pillars

锦江峡谷

Jinjiang Gorge

锦江峡谷：深切峡谷
Jinjiang Gorge: deep-cutting gorge

　　锦江峡谷的形成源于1,000年前的长白山火山爆发，爆发形成的火山碎屑流堆积物、浮岩和火山灰堆积物，在地壳抬升和流水侵蚀切割的联合作用下，形成了罕见的V型深切峡谷。峡谷平均宽度100米，最宽处达300米，平均谷深87米，最深处达160米。谷底与谷壁之上是茂密的原始森林，古树参天，巨石错落。峡谷中火山碎屑构成的微地貌景观，形态各异、奇景迭出，如"犀牛望月""骆驼双峰"。

The form a tion of Jinjiang Gorge originated from the large volcanic eruption of Mt. Changbaishan about 1,000 years ago. Under the combined effects of crustal uplift and water cutting along fractures, the pyroclastic flow deposits, pumice, and volcanic ash deposits formed by the volcanic eruption developed into a rare deeply incised V-shaped gorge. The gorge has an average width of 100 meters, reaching up to 300 meters at its widest point, with an average depth of 87 meters and a maximum depth of 160 meters. The vast primeval forest with ancient trees and scattered giant rocks covers the gorge floor and walls. The micro-landscapes formed by pyroclastic debris in the gorge are diverse and spectacular, resembling "a rhinoceros gazing at the moon" or "twin peaks of a camel", presenting a myriad of breathtaking sights.

冰雪覆盖的锦江峡谷
Jinjiang Gorge covered with ice and snow

锦江峡谷之夏
Jinjiang Gorge in summer

鸭绿江峡谷
Yalu River Gorge

鸭绿江峡谷

Yalu River Gorge

鸭绿江峡谷位于长白山南坡、距离天池30,000米的原始森林中，峡谷段长1,000米，宽200余米，深170余米。峡谷成因是1,000多年前火山爆发形成的火山碎屑物堆积在原来的沟谷和洼地中，后在地壳抬升和流水侵蚀切割的作用下，形成了典型的V型峡谷地貌。峡谷两壁未被侵蚀的坚硬物质形成了各种形态的石柱、石林，矗立在峡谷中，非常壮观。

The Yalu River Gorge is located in the primeval forest on the south slope of Mt. Changbaishan, 30,000 meters away from Lake Tianchi. The gorge section is 1,000 meters in length, more than 200 meters in width, and over 170 meters in depth. Its formation was due to the pyroclastic accumulation from the volcanic eruption 1,000 years ago in the original valleys and depressions. Later, under the combined effects of crustal uplift and water erosion and incision, a typical V-shaped gorge landform was formed. The hard materials on both walls of the gorge that have not been eroded have formed various shapes of stone column and stone forests standing in the valley, exhibiting diverse and spectacular forms.

鸭绿江峡谷
Yalu River Gorge

鸭绿江峡谷
Yalu River Gorge

森林生态
Forest Ecology

长白山上的生物都遵循着四季更迭和生命循环，春天的喧嚣并不是开始，冬天的萧索也不是结束。这里保存有亚洲东部最为完整的典型森林生态系统，森林木材总量约为7.1亿立方米，在生态系统年固碳、减少水土流失和承载水资源等方面发挥着巨大的作用。

All the organisms on Mt. Changbaishan follow the cycle of four seasons and life. The hustle and bustle of spring is not the beginning, and the desolation of winter is not the end. Here preserves the most intact and typical forest ecosystem in eastern Asia, with a total forest timber volume of approximately 710 million cubic meters. This ecosystem plays a crucial role in annual carbon sequestration, reducing soil erosion, and carrying water resources in the ecosystem.

动物资源

Animal Resources

　　野生动物是生物的一大类群，全世界约有150万种。其中，中国的野生有脊椎动物约6,000种，野生无脊椎动物20多万种；吉林省野生有脊椎动物约560种，野生无脊椎动物约4,400种；长白山区野生有脊椎动物约550种，野生无脊椎动物约3,900种。

　　Wildlife is a major group of organisms, with approximately 1.5 million species worldwide. China alone is home to over 6,000 species of wild vertebrates and more than 200,000 species of wild invertebrates. Jilin Province has over 560 species of wild vertebrates and more than 4,400 species of wild invertebrates. In Mt. Changbaishan, there are over 550 species of wild vertebrates and more than 3,900 species of wild invertebrates.

雪貂Mustela putorius furo

狍子Capreolus pygargus

猞猁Lynx

紫貂Martes zibellina

马鹿Cervus elaphus

棕熊Ursus arctos

花鼠Tamias sibiricus

林蛙Rana amurensis Boulenger

鸳鸯Aix galericulata

沼泽山雀Poecile palustris

太平鸟Bombycilla garrulus

柳莺Phylloscopus

渡鸦Corvus corax

戴胜Upupa epops

花尾榛鸡Bonasa bonasia

长尾林鸮Strix uralensis

雕鸮Bubo bubo

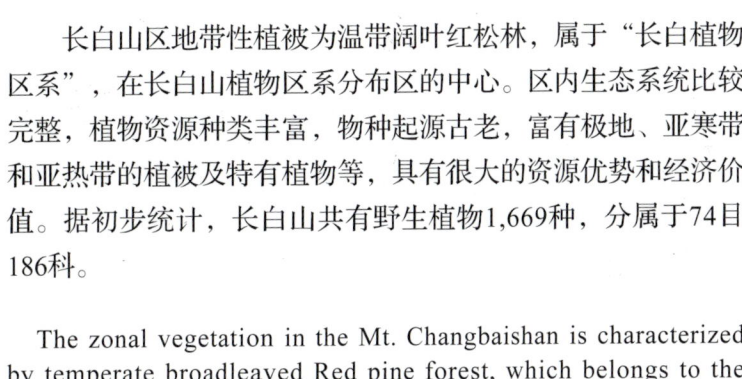

植物资源
Plant Resources

长白山区地带性植被为温带阔叶红松林，属于"长白植物区系"，在长白山植物区系分布区的中心。区内生态系统比较完整，植物资源种类丰富，物种起源古老，富有极地、亚寒带和亚热带的植被及特有植物等，具有很大的资源优势和经济价值。据初步统计，长白山共有野生植物1,669种，分属于74目186科。

The zonal vegetation in the Mt. Changbaishan is characterized by temperate broadleaved Red pine forest, which belongs to the "Changbai flora" and is the center of the "flora" distribution area of Mt. Changbaishan. The ecosystems in the area are relatively intact, with abundant plant resources and ancient origins. It is rich in vegetation from polar, subfrigid, and subtropical regions, as well as unique plants, providing significant resource advantages and economic value. According to preliminary statistics, there are a total of 1, 669 species of wild plants in Mt. Changbaishan, which belong to 74 orders and 186 families.

中华金腰Chrysosplenium sinicum Maxim

长白红景天Rhodiola angusta Nakai

侧金盏花Adonis amurensis Regel et Radde

温泉瓶尔小草Ophioglossum thermale Kom

库页红景天Rhodiola sachalinensis

枸兰Cypripedium calceolus L

斑花枸兰Cypripedium guttatum Swartz

圆叶茅膏菜Drosera rotundifolia L

长白岩菖蒲Tofieldia coccinea Rich

丝瓣剪秋萝Lychnis wilfordii (Regel) Maxim

球果假水晶兰
Cheilotheca humilis (D.Don) H.Kengin

细叶杜香Ledum palustre L

长白乌头Aconitum tschangbaischanense

长白岩黄耆Hedysarum ussuriensis
Schischk. et Kom

白花刺蔷薇Rosa acicularis Lindl. f. alba Z.
Wang et Q. L. Wang

野蓟Cirsium maackii Maxim

高山罂粟Papaver alpinum

苞叶杜鹃Rhododendron bracteatum

长白棘豆Oxytropis anertii Nakai

小山菊Chrysanthemum zawadskii Herbich
var. alpinum (Nakai) Kitam

笃斯越橘Vaccinium uliginosum L

补天石
Butian Stone

地质科学与科普
Geological Research

　　依托独特的火山地质地貌和森林生态资源，以地学旅游为龙头的全域旅游产业有力推动了当地社会经济的发展。长白山世界地质公园缔结合作伙伴，大力开展火山地质、生态保护等方面的科普教育和研学活动，建立火山博物馆，设立科普教育基地，开设火山科普网站，出版科普读物，让公众切实感受到自然的神奇和科学的魅力。

　　By leveraging Mt. Changbaishan's unique volcanic geological landforms and forest ecological resources, the comprehensive tourism industry led by geoscience tourism has significantly promoted local socio-economic development. Mt. Changbaishan UNESCO Global Geopark has forged partnerships and vigorously conducted popular science education and study tours related to volcanic geology, ecological conservation, etc. It has established a volcanic museum as well as set up popular science education bases. Besides, a volcanic popular science website has been launched and science books has been published. By conducting these plans, Mt. Changbaishan UNESCO Global Geopark is committed to enabling the public to truly experience the wonders of nature and the charm of science.

地质科考、勘测、交流等活动
Geological survey, exploration and exchange activities

地质科普、教育、研学活动

Geological popularization, education and research activities

四里洞洞口A

Entrance A of Sili Cave

四里洞洞口B

Entrance B of Sili Cave

四里洞内紧贴洞壁的碎屑流

Pyroclastic flow against the wall in Sili Cave

四里洞内顶板凝结的水珠

Water droplets condensed on the roof of
Sili Cave

四里洞内火山碎屑流贴在洞壁上形
成的剪切层理

Shear bedding formed by pyroclastic flow
against the wall in Sili Cave

四里洞内无根喷火口

Rootless volcanic vent inside Sili Cave

四里洞内的火山碎屑流堆积

Pyroclastic flows accumulated in Sili Cave

四里洞内火山碎屑流中的喷气孔

Fumarole in pyroclastic flows in Sili Cave

四里洞内碎屑流堆积物形成的小泥
火山口

Small mud craters formed by pyroclastic
flow deposits in Sili Cave

熔岩隧道

Lava Tunnel

　　火山熔岩隧道又称熔岩洞，是火山喷发时喷出的岩浆在流动过程中表层岩浆与空气接触先凝固，内部岩浆后续流动不足而形成的空洞。经勘探人员踏查和确认的熔岩隧道目前共有两处，分别是鹿蹄洞熔岩隧道和四里洞熔岩隧道。

　　The volcanic lava tunnel, also referred to as lava cave, is a cavity formed during volcanic eruptions when the surface layer of magma solidifies upon contact with the air. This process leaves behind a cavity due to insufficient flow of magma underneath. Currently, exploration teams have confirmed the existence of two lava tunnels: the Lava Tunnel of Luti Cave and the Lava Tunnel of Sili Cave.

冰场期凝灰岩（120,000年）
Tuff formed during the Ice Rink Period
(120,000 years)

锦江峡谷凝灰岩
Jinjiang Gorge tuff

气象站层状熔岩（8,200年）
Layered lava at the meteorological station
(8,200 years)

气象站黑曜质熔岩（8,200年）
Black obsidian lava at the meteorological
station (8,200 years)

气象站碱流质熔岩（8,200年）
Alkaline lava at the meteorological station
(8,200 years)

千年大喷发粗面质浮岩（967年）
Coarse pumice rocks from the Millennium
Eruption (967 years)

千年大喷发碱流质浮岩（946年）
Alkaline liquid pumice rocks from the
Millennium Eruption (946 years)

千年大喷发内的岩浆混合
Mixture of magma during the Millennium
Eruption

天文峰期黄色浮岩（50,000年）
Yellow pumice rocks from the Astronomy
Peak period (50,000 years)

火山灰包裹的炭化木
Carbonized wood covered with volcanic ash

炭化木遗迹
Carbonized Wood Remains

　　长白山炭化木遗迹是1,000多年前火山喷发产生的大量灼热的火山灰和浮石等火山碎屑物灼烧森林，树木炭化后保存在火山碎屑层中形成的。上图中的炭化木长约1米，顺火山碎屑层排列。

　　The charcoalized wood remains of Mt. Changbaishan can date back to 1,000 years ago when a volcanic eruption generated a large amount of scorching pyroclastic debris such as volcanic ash and pumice stones that burned the forest. These remains are formed and preserved within the layers of pyroclastic debris. The charcoalized wood found here has a length of approximately 1 meter. These remnants are often found arranged along the layers of pyroclastic debris.

长白山神庙遗址

Relic of Mt. Changbaishan Holy Temple

　　长白山神庙遗址位于长白山世界地质公园北端的宝马村。遗址近长方形，南北长约140米，东西宽约120米。长白山神庙由金代王族修建，该遗址是中原地区以外首次通过考古发现的国家级山祭遗存，其对探索金代礼仪制度的发展具有十分重要的意义，目前是长白山地区发现的保存最完好、等级最高的文化遗存。2017年长白山神庙遗址被列为"全国十大考古新发现"，2019年10月入选第八批全国重点文物保护单位名单。

　　Located in Baoma Village at the northern end of the Mt. Changbaishan UNESCO Global Geopark, the site of Mt. Changbaishan Holy Temple is approximately rectangular, with a length of about 140 meters from north to south and a width of about 120 meters from east to west. Built by the royal family during the Jin Dynasty, the site represents the first national-level mountain sacrifice site discovered through archaeology outside of the Central Plains. Currently, as the best-preserved and highest-ranked cultural relic discovered in the Mt. Changbaishan, the site holds significant importance in exploring the development of ritual systems during the Jin Dynasty. In 2017, the site was listed among the "Top Ten New Archaeological Discoveries in China". In October 2019, it was included in the eighth batch of National Key Cultural Relic Protection Units.

生态保护
Ecological Conservation

　　1960年成立的吉林省长白山自然保护区，是中华人民共和国成立以来建立的具有重要地位的森林生态类型自然保护区之一。建区60多年来，在吉林省委、省政府的高度重视和正确领导下，几代长白山人坚持"生态优先、保护第一"的原则，积极开展资源保护和森林防火工作，经过不懈努力，使长白山自然保护区生态环境持续改善，森林生态系统与生物多样性得到有效保护，实现建区以来连续60年无重大森林火灾，多次获得全国森林防火先进单位、全国野生动植物保护先进集体、全国自然保护区先进集体、吉林省森林防火模范单位等荣誉。

The Mt. Changbaishan National Nature Reserve, established in 1960 in Jilin Province, is one of the significant forest ecological-type nature reserves established since the founding of the People's Republic of China. Over the past 60 years, under the attentive leadership of the Jilin Provincial Party Committee and Provincial Government, generations of people dedicated to Mt. Changbaishan have adhered to the principle of "ecological priority, protection first", diligently carrying out resource conservation and forest fire prevention. Through unremitting efforts, the ecological environment of Mt. Changbaishan has continuously improved, and the forest ecosystem and biodiversity have been effectively protected. Since its establishment, the reserve has experienced no major forest fires for 60 consecutive years, and has been awarded numerous honors, including National Advanced Unit of Forest Fire Prevention, National Advanced Collective for Wildlife Protection, National Advanced Collective for Nature Reserves, and the Model Unit of Forest Fire Prevention in Jilin Province.

长白山森林公安局、武警森警部队长白山大队联合开展的反盗猎、反盗伐宣传车队

Anti-poaching and anti-logging publicizing convoys launched by the Mt. Changbaishan Forest Public Security Bureau and the Mt. Changbaishan Brigade of the Armed and Forest Police Force

长白山自然博物馆举办自然科普活动

Nature education activities organized by the Mt. Changbaishan Nature History Museum

科研人员在进行野外科研调查 (1)

Researchers conducting field research investigations (1)

科研人员在进行野外科研调查 (2)

Researchers conducting field research investigations (2)

长白山自然保护管理中心组织春季森林防火演练

The Mt. Changbaishan Nature Reserve Management Center was organizing spring forest fire prevention drill

2020国家自然保护地联盟成员大会在长白山召开

The 2020 IAPA General Assembly was held in Mt. Changbaishan

国际自然保护区联盟年会在长白山召开（2016）

The International Union for Conservation of Nature (IUCN) held its annual meeting in Mt. Changbaishan (2016)

第十三届世界人与生物圈东亚网络会议期间长白山保护区与俄罗斯锡霍特阿林保护区签署合作协议

A cooperation agreement was signed between Mt. Changbaishan Nature Reserve and Sikhot Alin Reserve in Russia during the 13th East Asia Network Conference on Man and the Biosphere

联合国教科文组织驻华代表处与长白山保护区共同主办的"人与生物圈计划青年论坛"上联合国教科文组织副总干事曲星在开幕式上发言

Qu Xing, Deputy Director-General of UNESCO, was speaking at the opening ceremony of the Youth Forum on Man and the Biosphere Program, which was co-hosted by Mt. Changbaishan and UNESCO Beijing Office

长白山代表团赴美国阿拉斯加考察并召开合作年会（2015）

A delegation of Mt. Changbaishan visited Alaska in USA for research and held an annual cooperation meeting (2015)

原国家林业局组织国际专家考察长白山保护区（2009）

The former State Forestry Administration organized international experts to investigate Mt. Changbaishan Nature Reserve (2009)

长白山保护区工作人员赴美国卡克托维克野生生物庇护所实地参与欧绒鸭调查

Staff from Mt. Changbaishan Nature Reserve visited Kaktovik Wildlife Sanctuary in the United States to participate in a survey on Steller's eiders

全域旅游

Holistic Tourism

　　长白山保护开发区管理委员会立足于长白山的地质地貌、森林生态、水文气象等方向的基础研究，建成了集资源保护、科研教学、自然教育和地学旅游为一体的综合性地质公园。完善的旅游基础设施，发达的立体交通网络，围绕地质生态、休闲康养、冰雪运动、研学科普打造的全链条旅游业态，使每年有200多万的游客慕名而来。

The Mt. Changbaishan Protection and Development Zone Management Committee, based on the foundational research of Mt. Changbaishan' geological landscape, forest ecology, hydrology, and meteorology, has built this territory into a comprehensive geopark integrating with resources protection, scientific research and teaching, nature education and geotourism. The sound tourism infrastructure and well-developed transportation network have provided a firm foundation for the Geopark as an attracting destination for geological and ecological studies, leisure and health care, ice and snow sports, and science research and popularization. Nowadays, the Geopark welcomes more than 2 million tourists every year.

城区风貌
Urban landscape

地质合作伙伴
Geological partners

125

池北景区

Introduction to Chibei Area

池北区是长白山天池火山的北坡区域，是地质遗迹与自然景观分布最多的一个区域。在这一区域，游客们可以深入神秘的谷底森林，探秘由熔岩塌陷和流水下切作用形成的谷底风景；可以登上两座奇峰交会的黑风口，瞭望壮丽的长白瀑布——松花江源头；更可以历览从温带到极地的植被更替，然后一路攀上天文峰，欣赏如仙境般的火山口湖——天池。此外还有小天池、绿渊潭、聚龙温泉等各具特色的地质与自然景观。

The Chibei Area lies on the north slope of Lake Tianchi of Mt. Changbaishan, with most abundant and various geological and natural landforms. In this area, visitors can delve into the miraculous forest at the valley bottom to explore unusual scenery formed by the lava collapse and fluvial down-cutting; visitors can also climb up to the Heifengkou, the intersection of two magic peaks, enjoying the magnificent Changbai Waterfall—the source of Songhua River; and also one can experience the alternation of vegetations from the temperate to polar floras along the mountaineering way. When climbing up to the summit of Astronomy Peak, one can sight the fairyland—Lake Tianchi—a summit crater lake. In addition, there are Little Lake Tianchi, Luyuan Pool, Julong Hot Sping and other geological and natural spots in this area.

池西景区

Introduction to Chixi Area

　　池西区是长白山天池火山的西坡区域。在此区域内，有罕见的高原火山成因峡谷地貌——锦江大峡谷。锦江大峡谷形成于长白山千年大喷发的火山碎屑堆积物上，是由地壳抬升和水流切割形成的深切峡谷，保留了长白山喷发过程的详细记录和世界上独特的石林、石柱，以及象形的微地貌景观。还有由流水沿玄武岩节理和缝隙下切侵蚀而成的两壁陡峭、构造奇特的梯子河。游客还可游览王池等火山口湖、高山花园等，沿白云峰路线攀登而上，观赏从温带到极地的自然景观，探寻天池西侧的独特风景。

The Chixi Area is situated on the west slope of Lake Tianchi of Mt. Changbaishan. Within this area lies the rare alpine volcanic-induced gorge — the Jinjiang Gorge, which is developed jointly by crust elevation and fluvial down-cutting on the pyroclastic accumulation during the massive eruption. It preserves the detailed record of the eruption process and world-unique and fantastic pyroclastic stone forest, columns and pictographic micro-landform. Visitors can enjoy the peculiar Tizihe River (literally meaning "ladder river") with steep cliffs on both banks, which was derived from the fluvial down-cutting along the joints or fissures in basalts. In addition, there are many other attractions, such as crater lakes (i.e., Lake Wangchi), alpine garden, and others. Besides, along the mountaineering route up to Peak Baiyun, one can enjoy the vegetation alternation from the temperate to polar regions and explore the unique landscapes on the west side of Lake Tianchi.

池南景区

Introduction to Chinan Area

池南区是长白山天池火山的南坡区域。在此区域内，游客可以看到大规模的炭化木遗迹，还有罕见的高原火山碎屑峡谷地貌——鸭绿江大峡谷，景色十分壮美。此外，游客们还可游览高山湿地、岳华霜瀑、长白石林等，登山沿途可观赏从温带到极地的植被交替，探寻天池南侧的独特风景。

The Chinan Area is located on the south slope of the Lake Tianchi of Mt. Changbaishan. Within this area, visitors can observe the unusual carbonized woods. Visitors can enjoy the alpine pyroclastic gorge—the Yalu River Gorge. The other sites include the alpine wetland, Yuehuashuang Waterfall, Changbai Stone Forest. Besides, one can also enjoy the vegetation alternation from the temperate to polar regions along the mountaineering route and explore the unique landscapes on the south side of Lake Tianchi.

建设生态文明 实现绿色发展

Ecological Civilization and Green Development

　　长白山有着探索不完的奥秘，在这里，火山地貌与冰川遗迹同生共存，高山花园与莽莽雪山刚柔相济，众多民族与自然生态和谐共生。

　　长白山及其天池、瀑布、雪雕、林海等曾多次入选吉尼斯世界纪录，有中华十大名山、中国最美的五大湖泊、中国最美的十大森林等美誉。更在2024年3月通过联合国教科文组织评选，跻身"世界地质公园"行列，成为吉林省首座世界地质公园，更加表明了长白山在生态、生物、地质和历史等诸多方面都具有突出的普遍价值和卓越的自然品质，以及丰富的文化内涵。

　　Mt. Changbaishan, abundant with mysteries to be explored, is a place where volcanic landforms and glacial remnants coexist, where alpine gardens and vast snow-covered mountains complement each other, and where many ethnic groups live in harmony with the natural ecology.

　　Mt. Changbaishan, along with its Lake Tianchi, cascading waterfalls, intricate snow sculptures, and lush forests, has garnered international recognition through multiple entries in the Guinness World Records for various accomplishments. It has earned titles such as one of China's Top Ten Famous Mountains, one of China's Five Most Beautiful lakes, and one of China's Ten Most Beautiful Forests and ect. Additionally, in March 2024, it is designated as a "Global Geopark" by UNESCO, marking it as the first of its kind in Jilin Province. These awards further underscore Mt. Changbaishan's outstanding universal value and remarkable natural qualities, and profound cultural significance in terms of ecology, biology, geology, history and ect.

图书在版编目（CIP）数据

大美长白山：汉、英 / 卓永生，孙志主编. -- 长
春：吉林科学技术出版社，2024.5
ISBN 978-7-5744-1283-5

Ⅰ.①大… Ⅱ.①卓… ②孙… Ⅲ.①长白山—旅游
指南—汉、英 Ⅳ.①K928.3

中国国家版本馆CIP数据核字(2024)第087334号

大美长白山
DA MEI CHANGBAI SHAN

主　　编	卓永生　孙　志
出 版 人	宛　霞
责任编辑	赵渤婷
封面设计	长春市吾擅文化传媒有限公司
制　　版	长春美印图文设计有限公司
幅面尺寸	210 mm×260 mm
开　　本	16
印　　张	8.5
字　　数	320千字
版　　次	2024年5月第1版
印　　次	2024年5月第1次印刷

出　　版　吉林科学技术出版社
发　　行　吉林科学技术出版社
地　　址　长春市福祉大路5788号出版大厦A座
邮　　编　130118
发行部电话/传真　0431-81629529　81629530　81629531
　　　　　　　　　　81629532　81629533　81629534
储运部电话　0431-86059116
编辑部电话　0431-81629518
印　　刷　吉林省吉广国际广告股份有限公司

书　　号　ISBN 978-7-5744-1283-5
定　　价　298.00元

如有印装质量问题　可寄出版社调换
版权所有　翻印必究　举报电话：0431-81629508

《大美长白山》项目组委员会

Great Beauty of Mt. Changbaishan Project Committee

项目组委员会

主　　任：李志宏

副 主 任：孟凡迎　徐连翔

委　　员：沈　婷　葛平南　付志国　艾贵生　邵明智

　　　　　王　琳　孙　志　王　萌　孔繁伟　张荣杰

　　　　　赵月明

文　　字：卓永生　赫兰辉　胡婷婷　张文强

翻　　译：北京必睿国际文化传播有限公司

摄　　影：卓永生　武成智　朴龙国　朴永吉

科学顾问：张建平　牛丽君

视频专题创作人员

总策划：高　飞

总监制：李志宏

策　划：徐连翔

导　演：卓永生　张建平

撰　稿：卓永生　潘　波　武成智

摄　像：卓永生　张秋森

翻　译：张建平　李雨欣

配　音：盛锡友

剪　辑：王　萌　周　徽　金　磊

合　成：王　琳　孔繁伟

技　术：王英民

科学指导：张建平　武成智

制　片：沈　婷　葛平南

监　制：孟凡迎

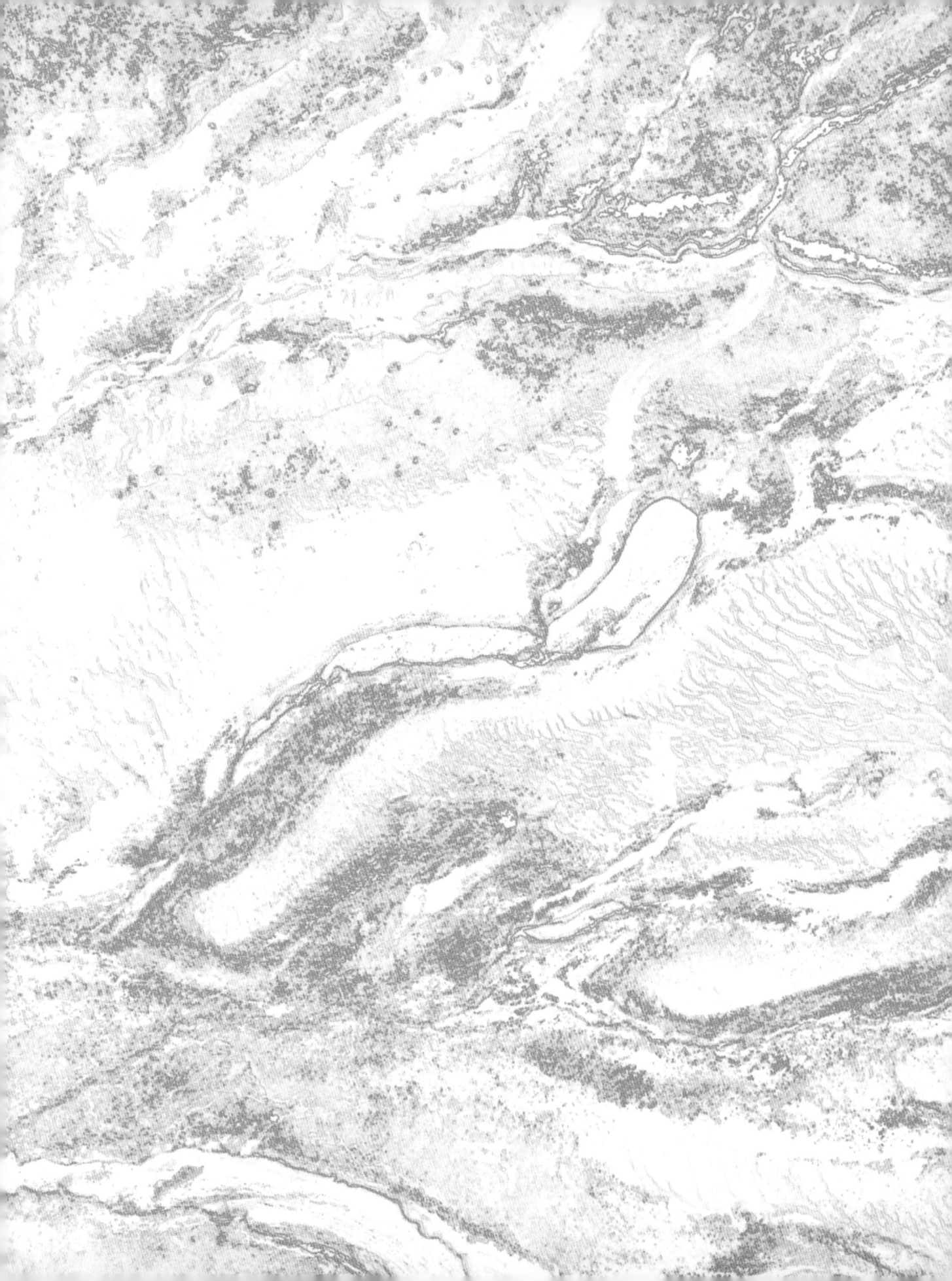